Finding Patterns

People Patterns

by Nathan Olson

Capstone press®

Mankato, Minnesota

A+ Books are published by Capstone Press,
151 Good Counsel Drive, P.O. Box 669, Mankato, Minnesota 56002.
www.capstonepress.com

1 2 3 4 5 6 12 11 10 09 08 07

Library of Congress Cataloging-in-Publication Data
Olson, Nathan.
   People patterns / by Nathan Olson.
   p. cm.—(A+ books. Finding patterns)
   Summary: "Simple text and color photographs introduce different kinds of people patterns"–Provided by publisher.
   Includes bibliographical references and index.
   ISBN-13: 978-0-7368-6731-3 (hardcover)
   ISBN-10: 0-7368-6731-7 (hardcover)
   ISBN-13: 978-0-7368-7849-4 (softcover pbk.)
   ISBN-10: 0-7368-7849-1 (softcover pbk.)
   1. Pattern perception—Juvenile literature. 2. Human beings—Miscellanea—Juvenile literature. I. Title. II. Series.
   BF294.O55 2007
   516'.15—dc22   2006018191

Credits

Jenny Marks, editor; Renée Doyle, designer; Charlene Deyle, photo researcher; Scott Thoms, photo editor

Photo Credits

Corbis/Bob Krist, 14; Corbis/epa/EPA/Harish Taygi, 12; Corbis/Jeremy Horner, 4–5; Corbis/Justin Guariglia, 22; Corbis Sygma/Pierre Vauthey, 10–11; Corbis/zefa/Adrianna Williams, 15; Corbis/zefa/Hugh Sitton, 16; Corbis/zefa/Pete Saloutos, 24; Getty Images Inc./Blend Images/Ariel Skelley, cover (girl); Getty Images Inc./Iconica/Zia Soleil, 26–27; Getty Images Inc./Photonica/Rana Faure, 7; Getty Images Inc./Reportage/Chris Hondros, 23; Getty Images Inc./Stone/Bob Torrez, 8–9; Getty Images Inc./Stone/GDT, 19; Getty Images Inc./Stone/Rene Sheret, 13; Getty Images Inc./Taxi/Ken Chernus, 20–21; Getty Images Inc./The Image Bank/Darren Robb, 6; PhotoEdit Inc./Dennis MacDonald, 17; Richard Cummins, 25; Shutterstock/Larry St. Pierre, 29; Shutterstock/Linda Webb, cover (waves); Shutterstock/Suzanne Tucker, 18

Note to Parents, Teachers, and Librarians

Finding Patterns uses color photographs and a nonfiction format to introduce readers to seeing patterns in the real world. *People Patterns* is designed to be read aloud to a pre-reader, or to be read independently by an early reader. Images and activities encourage mathematical thinking in early readers and listeners. The book encourages further learning by including the following sections: Table of Contents, People Pattern Facts, Glossary, Read More, Internet Sites, and Index. Early readers may need assistance using these features.

Table of Contents

What Is a Pattern?............................4

Wearing Patterns.........................10

Action Patterns............................22

People Pattern Facts...................28

Glossary......................................30

Read More 31

Internet Sites 31

Index 32

What Is a Pattern?

A pattern is made when shapes and colors repeat. Let's look for patterns people make every day.

A line of boy, girl, boy, girl makes an every-other pattern.

But boys and girls playing together don't always make a pattern.

All-the-same makes a pattern too. Identical triplets are a natural-born pattern.

Wearing Patterns

Spots called polka dots are same-size circles. Wearing lots of dots makes a pattern.

Soldiers in India wear a special pattern of stripes and folds on their hats.

Chefs wear hats with a plainer pattern. But just look at their fancy food patterns!

You can wear every-other patterns in your hair. How many patterns do you see in these colorful beads?

These fancy painted fingernails have a red and white polish pattern.

Tattoos can make permanent patterns. The shapes and pictures sometimes tell stories or have special meanings.

For powwows and other tribal events, Ojibwa children wear clothes decorated with patterns of colors and shapes.

Referees wear a striped pattern that's easy to see.

Fans wear stripes too. Their white and blue face paint makes playful patterns.

What winning pattern
does this team wear?

Action Patterns

Rows of kung fu students practice the same movement pattern.

Left! Right! Left! A marching line of uniformed cadets makes a pattern.

A wheel pattern shimmers
when swimmers join their
hands and feet.

A red, white, and blue band performs a tune while standing in a pattern.

Everyone, give a cheer for the patterns people make!

People Pattern Facts

Chef's hats have a purpose other than keeping hair out of food. Each hat has a pattern of tiny pleats around it. More pleats means a higher-ranking chef. Some chef's hats have 100 pleats, meaning the wearer is the top chef in the kitchen.

The Queen's Guard is a group of military men who guard the royal palaces in the United Kingdom. These palace guards wear uniforms of red, black, and white. Royal guard members never speak or smile while they are on duty.

Jingle dances are traditionally done by American Indian women at gatherings called powwows. Jingle dance dresses have a pattern of seven rows of cone-shaped bells. Dancers move with a slow rhythm that causes the bells to swing and jingle.

Native people in New Zealand once used tattoos to show their status in the tribe. As a Maori tribesman became more important in the tribe, he added to the tattoo pattern. The highest level of Maori tattoo was reserved for the tribe's chief.

A polka dot pattern is made up of dots the same size and distance apart. Polka dots became common on clothing in Great Britain in the late 1800s. At about the same time, German polka music was popular. Some people think the popularity of polka music gave polka dots their name.

Referees make sure that sports players follow the rules. They wear black-and-white striped shirts so that players can easily spot them on the playing field.

Glossary

cadet (kuh-DET)—a young person who is training
to become a member of the armed forces
or a police force

chef (SHEF)—the head cook in a restaurant

identical (eye-DEN-ti-kuhl)—exactly alike

kung fu (KUHNG FOO)—one of the Chinese
martial arts practiced for exercise and
self-defense

permanent (PUR-muh-nuhnt)—lasting for a long
time or forever

polka dot (POKE-uh DOT)—one of many same-sized
dots that are repeated to form a pattern

referee (ref-uh-REE)—someone who supervises
a sports match or game and makes sure that
the players obey the rules

tattoo (ta-TOO)—a picture that has been printed
onto a person's skin with pigments
and needles

triplet (TRIP-lit)—one of three children born
at the same time to the same mother

Read More

Boothroyd, Jennifer. *Patterns.* First Step Nonfiction. Minneapolis: LernerClassroom, 2007.

Hammersmith, Craig. *Patterns.* Spyglass Books. Minneapolis: Compass Point Books, 2003.

Pistoia, Sara. *Patterns.* MathBooks. Chanhassen, Minn.: Child's World, 2006.

Internet Sites

FactHound offers a safe, fun way to find Internet sites related to this book. All of the sites on FactHound have been researched by our staff.

Here's how:

1. Go to *www.facthound.com*
2. Select your grade level.
3. Type in this book **ID 0736867317** for age-appropriate sites. You may also browse subjects by clicking on the letters, or by clicking on pictures and words.
4. Click on the **Fetch It** button.

FactHound will fetch the best sites for you!

Index

all-the-same patterns, 9

cadets, 23

chefs, 13, 28

color patterns, 5, 14, 15, 17, 19, 25, 28, 29

every-other patterns, 6, 14

folds, 12

hats, 12, 13, 28

lines, 6, 23

pleats, 13, 28

polka dots, 11, 29

powwows, 17, 28

rows, 22, 28

shape patterns, 5, 11, 16, 17, 28

stripes, 12, 18, 19, 29

tattoos, 16, 29

triplets, 9

wheel patterns, 24